W World Kids
WHAT IN THE WORLD IS AN
AFFIRMATION?

by Martina Marie Domino

What in the World is an Affirmation? by Martina Domino

©2023 Martina Domino Writes LLC

Cover design by Martina Marie Domino

ISBN: 979-8-218-24048-6

A MESSAGE TO READERS

Affirmations are short phrases you can repeat to change the way you think and feel about yourself. They promote positive thinking, self-esteem, and motivation. They are free and easy to practice anywhere.

This book was made to help kids like you have a positive and wonderful start to your day. It is light and is the perfect size to carry along in the car, your backpack, to school, or wherever you may go.

I hope you enjoy. Remember to love yourself and be positive...you have so much to offer the world!

I am CONFIDENT

I can do this

I am brave

I'm very PROUD — of me —

I am loved

I am amazing

I'm Feeling good

I am good

I love to love

I am kind

I can make a difference

I am beautiful

I bring peace

I deserve good things

CHECK OUT OTHER
W World Kids
BOOKS!

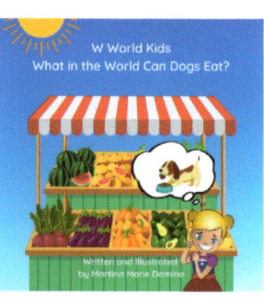
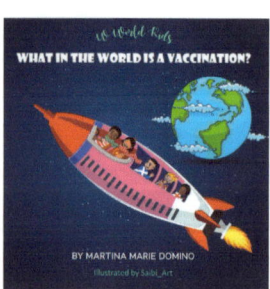

Visit: https://www.martinadomino.com

Instagram   Website   Facebook   Twitter

WHICH
W World Kid
IS YOUR FAVORITE!?

Drop a line and let me know!

Instagram   **Website**   **Facebook**   **Twitter**

www.ingramcontent.com/pod-product-compliance
Lightning Source LLC
Chambersburg PA
CBHW041745040426
42444CB00001B/31